MAESTRO PLEASE!

cartoons by
ED FISHER

APPLAUSE BOOKS

211 West 71st St, New York, NY 10023

MAESTRO PLEASE!

APPLAUSE BOOKS

211 West 71st St, New York, NY 10023

An Applause Original

MAESTRO, PLEASE!
Cartoons by Ed Fisher
Copyright © 1992 by Ed Fisher

Grateful Acknowledgment is made to *The New Yorker, Harper's Magazine, Punch, The Saturday Review, The Opera Quarterly,* and "TOPPIX" where many of these works originally appeared.

ISBN:1-55783-108-4

Library of Congress Cataloging-in-Publication Data
Fisher, Edwin.
  Maestro, please! : cartoons / by Ed Fisher
      p.   cm.
  "An Applause original."
  ISBN 1-55783-108-4 (pbk) : $7.95
  1. Music - - Caricatures and cartoons.
  2. American wit and humor,
Pictorial.   I. Title.
NC1429.F438A4 1991
741. 5'973- - dc20

APPLAUSE BOOKS
211 West 71st Street
New York, NY 10023
212-595-4735

This Applause title is available at quantity discounts for premium use by your organization. Please write to our Marketing division.

"Well, I **was** going to call this my **'Symphonie Pathètique'**, but now that I got the grant and all the publicity I'm renaming it 'Ode to Joy!' "

*"At least it's better than those
awful radios."*

"...And now, the young composer's 'Persian Gulf Suite'..."

*"I don't find it easy playing — **or** living — 'Ein Heldenleben'!"*

"Before we start — has everybody practiced?"

*"That's his **third** flub!"*

"My wife thinks it's going to take me all night to write the 'Don Giovanni' overture — but I finished it hours ago."

*"Legalize drugs? Are you mad? Look what
happened when we legalized parallel fifths!"*

"Not 'Afternoon of Faun' again?"

*"**This** shell seems to have gone over to a New Age **interpretation** of the roaring-of-the-waves."*

COME IN!
AND TEST
OUR NEW
PIANOS

"Minimalist music, minimalist pay!"

"– And for my ability to enjoy this wonderful moment of triumph, I particularly want to thank Doctor Jeffrey Helmholtz, who helped me overcome a lifelong allergy to plants."

"When she said she'd had it with me, I was as stunned as if Alfred Brendel were to say he'd had it with Beethoven!"

"...And, according to Grove's Dictionary, this last song-cycle was written in an attempt by the composer to regain the favor of his patron, the Ford Foundation."

"I'll speak plainly. You want to import the oil.
We *want to export the band..."*

*"...But I can't hear what **you're** hearing, Norman. I can only hear the cello part."*

"Really, Franz. Ten years is a long time to spend writing something you intend to call an *'Impromptu.'* "

"I hear it! – complete to the last note as I fling it on
the page! The great sweeping glissandos, the violins
speaking of ecstacy, the brasses rolling on huge
chromatic swells! ... oh! It's something by Scriabin!"

"What do you mean, how come Satie is such a fad this year? How come **you** were such a fad last year?"

"– And afterwards the other one re-plays short excerpts and gives a little lecture of explanation."

"No, we're Holsteins. Bösendörfer is a piano."

*"He certainly isn't letting any of us poor slobs
forget that this is the Beethoven Bicentennial Year."*

"Just because they sneered at Stravinsky doesn't mean I can't sneer at fifteen minutes of straight silence labeled 'Profound Interlude No. 2.'"

*"And what am **I** supposed to do to express my brooding insights?"*

"All during the Stalin years, Alexei, your father managed, secretly, to keep Soviet tap dancing alive."

"All I'm saying is that if there can be a 'Solisti New York' why can't there be a 'Solisti New Jersey'?"

"You're fit enough to continue doing the slave's chorus in 'Nabucco', but I'd definitely caution against doing the anvil chorus in 'Trovatore'!"

*"He may not have your god-like beauty, but he's got plenty of **das Reingold!**"*

"She plays Carmen – but I can't remember if it's
in the Peter Brook Carmen, the Frank Corsaro
Carmen, the Frank Rosi Carmen, the Godard
Carmen or that Spanish ballet-movie Carmen."

*"Shall I press **roof**?"*

"I don't like this tampering with the score. He should be using an axe."

*"What has it got to to with your being a woman? I've been playing second fiddle all of **my** life too."*

"Those drums! Tap-tapping incessantly, with barely a change of timbre or rhythm! Do you suppose it could be something by Phillip Glass?"

*"Notice? – it's never the tubas or the violas or the tympani – it's always sh-sh-sh to **us**!"*

"Are you braced? Musicologists in Vienna have
turned up **another** biblical opera written in
declamatory 12-tone!"

"...Schubert's 'Winterreisen, Number Four'..."

"...And now a selection from the Musical, 'Hair'..."

*"This was our final all-Beethoven concert.
Hereafter, we will be performing as a rock group."*

"It's Ravel's 'Concerto for the Left Hand'."

"I go on playing, but sometimes I wonder if anyone is listening out there?"

"More cacaphony!"

*"Me, too. Out of veneration for Beethoven, I limited my output to nine symphonies – and now it turns out the son of a bitch wrote **ten** symphonies!"*

"I'll say it's the twilight of the Gods!"

*"But, Pythagorus, even if you **do** invent an eight-tone scale – what's to prevent some fool from inventing a **twelve**-tone scale?"*

"Get set! – And remember, every wrong note only adds to the impression that our great city is going down the drain!"

*"Look! – even **here** they're transcribing everything for flute!"*

*"Beg pardon, maestro, but when can we expect
'Madame Butterfly II'?"*

*"Think what a coup it would be: Aida and Radames sealed up in the tomb with nothing to eat except **our** client's cookies!"*

"...Now – molto vivace!..."

*"Let's see: that's fourteen coffees **fortissimo** on the milk, six of them **dolce**; eighteen teas, **pessante** on sugar, **ma non troppo** on the milk..."*

"Well, I don't really like to type myself or my material but if I had to I'd say I was basically carrying on the old bardic tradition originated in the Skandian-Celtic areas of Medieval Northern Europe."

"That lucky snake – being charmed by the entire Vienna Wind Octet."

*"What I was thinking was that maybe **we** could spur the East-West negotiations by proposing to the Bolshoi Company a balanced and mutual reduction in spear-carriers?"*

"Knock it off, Mac!"

"Well, frankly, Lloyd, I think the laugh is really on all those critics who called my 'Long Piece for Orchestra' a 'meaningless' work. In fact, it's really Beethoven's ninth played backwards."

"You have just heard the Second Brandenburg Concerto, performed by the Pro Harmonia Antigua Society under conditions similar to those prevailing at music festivals in the time of Bach."

*"I suppose Marsden has bragged to you about finally coming to terms with 'Falstaff' this year? – He knows this is the year everyone **else** is coming to terms with 'Electra'!"*

*"You know, in his sort of hifalutin, nutty way he's
touching on some mighty commonplace truths."*

"Remember, now – it's one, two, KICK, three, cha-cha-cha. One, two, KICK, three, cha-cha-cha."

*"Turn down that Serkin/Ormandy recording of
the Brahms Concerto Number Two!"*

*"They've re-done the acoustics here three times,
and I understand they're still lousy."*

"Ahoy, there! Can you give me an A?"

*"Beethoven is speaking! And **you're** not listening!"*

*"Yeah, I could've gone to heaven. But it would've meant I'd have to hang out with Brahms, Shubert, and **that** crowd!"*

"I wanted Pavarotti."

*"We've got to face it, Orlando. The kids today want
more fortissimos, appoggiaturas, grace-notes, trills..."*

"Gotterdammerung!"

*"...A Miss Trudy Vroome from Zappo Records in Los Angeles, with word that the Gregorian chant is '**in**' again."*

"I gave at the wind octet."

"Be warned: this story of ours might strain a lot of people's credulity, Mr. Wagner."

"Okay, boys! One more rousing Aristophanic chorus."

"It's Brava!"

"Hi. Would you like some romantic Gypsy violin music, arranged for flute?"

THE CAR OF ORPHEUS

*"Listen! – that's **our** protest song!"*

*"**Enough** nachtmusik!"*

"Now, Protons, at this point you reach critical mass."

"You can't win. Just when we could **use** a little
ethnic patronisation, suddenly they decide to
judge us by utterly impartial standards."

"Well, nice seeing you. Lots of luck and all that polyphony."

*"– About this next work to be performed, ladies and gentlemen: remember, these concerts are only **mostly** Mozart."*

"Easy, kid – not till the section marked 'molto espressivo.' "

2·20

"– And if you just press here, it plays Schubert's
'The Wanderer Fantasy.'"

*"Say, Captain, do you think we could get the
crew together for another of those marvelous
sea-chanteys?..."*

*"...On the contrary. I can't help thinking Wagner might have **liked** it."*

*"Now there **is** a rich man!"*